HISTORY FROM OBJECTS
IN THE
HOME

Karen Bryant-Mole

Wayland

HISTORY FROM OBJECTS

In The Home
Keeping Clean
At School
Toys
Clothes
In The Street

This edition published in 1996 by
Wayland (Publishers) Ltd

First published in 1994 by Wayland (Publishers) Ltd
61 Western Road, Hove, East Sussex, BN3 1JD, England

© Copyright 1994 Wayland (Publishers) Ltd

Edited by Deborah Elliott
Designed by Malcolm Walker

British Library Cataloguing in Publication Data
Bryant-Mole, Karen
   In the Home. - (History From Objects Series)
   I. Title II. Series
   643.09

HARDBACK ISBN 0-7502-1017-6

PAPERBACK ISBN 0-7502-1895-9

Typeset by Kudos Editorial and Design Services
Printed and bound in Italy by G. Canale & C. S.p.A.

Notes for parents and teachers
This book has been designed to be used on many different levels.

It can be used as a means of comparing and contrasting objects from the past with those of the present. Differences between the objects can be identified. Such differences might include the shape, colour or size of the objects.

It can be used to look at the way designs have developed as our knowledge and technology have improved. Children can consider the similarities between the objects and look at the way particular design features have been refined. They can look at the materials that the objects are made of and the way they work. Modern goods are often made of modern materials such as plastic. Older mechanical objects are now frequently powered by electricity.

The book can be used to help place objects in chronological order and to help children understand that development in design corresponds with a progression through time.

It can also be used to make deductions about the way people in the past lived their lives. Children can think about how and why the objects might have been used and who might have used them.

It is designed to show children that historical objects can reveal much about the past. At the same time it links the past with the present by showing that many of the familiar objects we use today have their roots firmly planted in history.

Contents

Some of the more difficult words which appear in **bold** are explained in the glossary on page 30.

Hot water bottles

We use hot water bottles to warm up our beds in winter.

1880s

This hot water bottle is made from stoneware. Stoneware is a type of pottery.
Hot water was poured in through the hole in the top and a stopper was put into the
hole to stop the water coming out.

4

1930s

Here is a hot water bottle made from aluminium. Aluminium is a metal, and metals get hot very easily.
A bed would soon have warmed up with this hot water bottle.

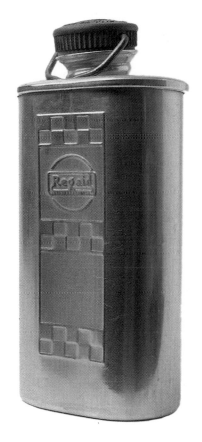

Now

Today we can buy hot water bottles with fun covers. The bottle inside this cover is made from rubber.
Stoneware and aluminium are hard **materials**, but this hot water bottle is warm and soft.

Kitchen scales

We use scales to weigh out **ingredients** when cooking.

1910s

There are a set of weights in front of these scales. The cook chose a weight and put it on the tray on the left. The ingredients were poured into the pan on the right until the two sides were the same level.

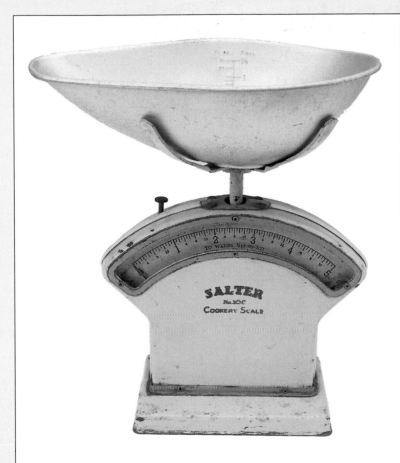

1930s

The ingredients were put into the pan on top of these scales.
The weight of the ingredients pushed down on the scales. This made the red arrow move to show the weight.

Now

These scales work using batteries. The scales measure the weight of the ingredients, and the weight is shown on the little screen.

Toasters

We use toasters to heat up bread and make it crispy and brown.

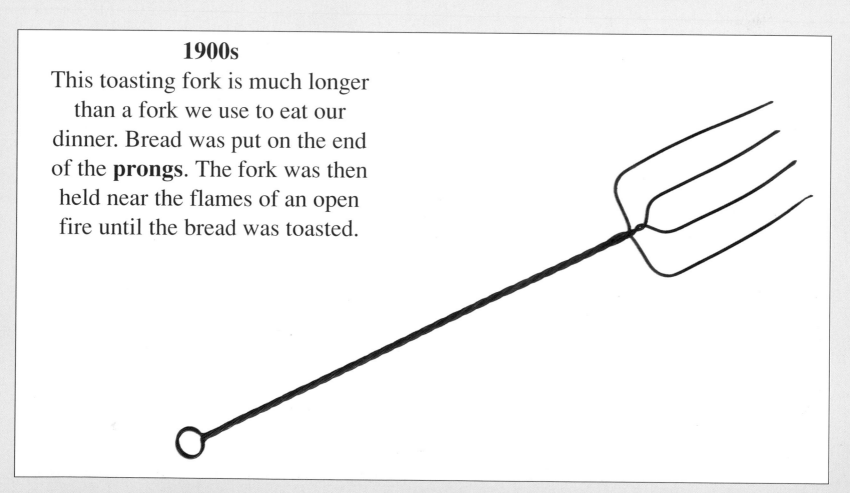

1900s

This toasting fork is much longer than a fork we use to eat our dinner. Bread was put on the end of the **prongs**. The fork was then held near the flames of an open fire until the bread was toasted.

1930s

This toaster was one of the first to work using electricity. It was easier to use than the toasting fork. The bread was laid against the sides which heated up and toasted the bread.

Now

The toasters we use today have special **settings**, which toast the bread to the right colour. The outside of the toaster is made of a special material which doesn't get too hot.

Can openers

Before can openers, people opened tins with a hammer and chisel!

1880s

This is one of the first can openers. The sharp point on the top made a hole in the tin. The blade was then used to cut around the top of the tin.
This can opener has a bull's head because it was used to open tins of canned beef.

1970s

This can opener was **clamped** on to the edge of the tin. As the handle was turned, a small round wheel, made from sharp steel, cut through the lid.

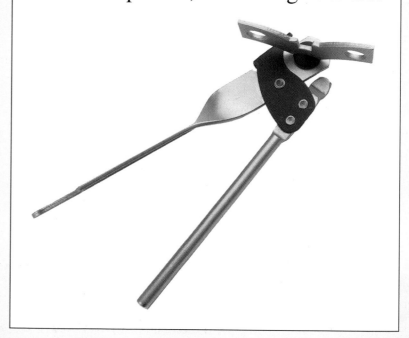

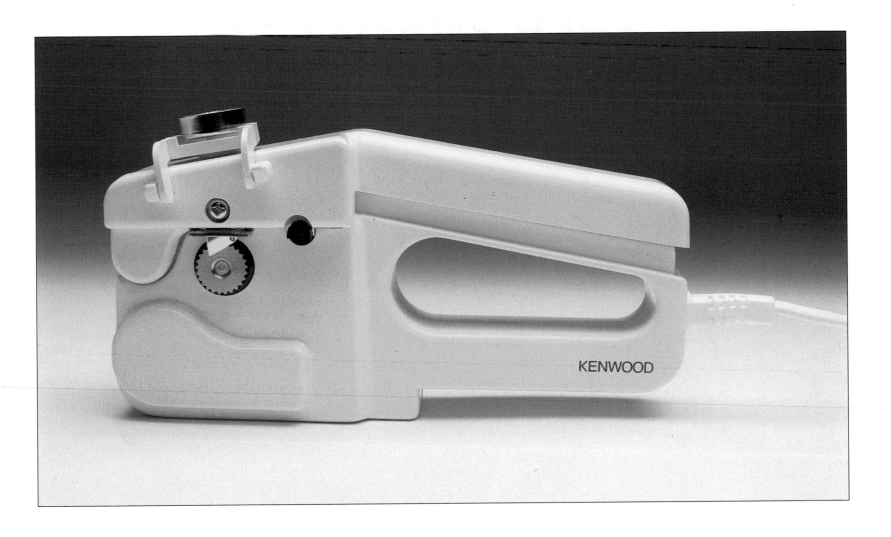

Now

This can opener works in the same way as the 1970s can opener, except that this one uses electricity.

It also has a **magnet** which holds on to the lid.

Fridges

We use fridges to keep food cool and fresh.

1900s

This is a very old fridge.
It is a wooden box,
lined with lead.

1920s

This is one of the first electric fridges. The machinery which keeps the food cool is in the bottom half of the fridge. So, food could only be kept in the top half of the fridge.

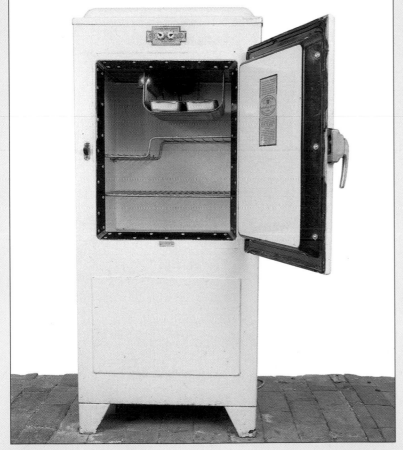

Now

The machinery in a modern fridge is very small and is all at the back of the fridge. This means food can be stored from the top of the fridge to the bottom - plenty of room for milk, eggs and yoghurt!

Beds and bedding

The most usual place for people to sleep is in a bed covered with blankets or a duvet.

1890s -1920s

This bed has a heavy, iron **frame**.

There are sheets and blankets on the bed. The blankets are covered by a patchwork quilt. Someone would have spent a long time sewing all the pieces of material together to make the patchwork quilt.

Now

This bed has a wooden frame. There are wooden drawers and a wooden cupboard under the bed where toys and clothes are kept. The person who sleeps in this bed has a duvet instead of blankets. Duvets are filled with feathers or nylon. The duvet cover can be taken off and washed.

Cookers

Before cookers, people cooked food on open fires. This must have been quite dangerous.

1860s

This type of cooker is called a range. A small coal fire in the **grate** at the bottom of the range heated up the two ovens and the hot plates on top.

1930s

Gas was used to heat the oven and the rings on this cooker. Someone had to light the gas with a match.

Now

This cooker has two parts; the oven and the **hob**. There is a grill inside the oven. Both the oven and the hob are heated by electricity.

Kettles

We use kettles to boil water.

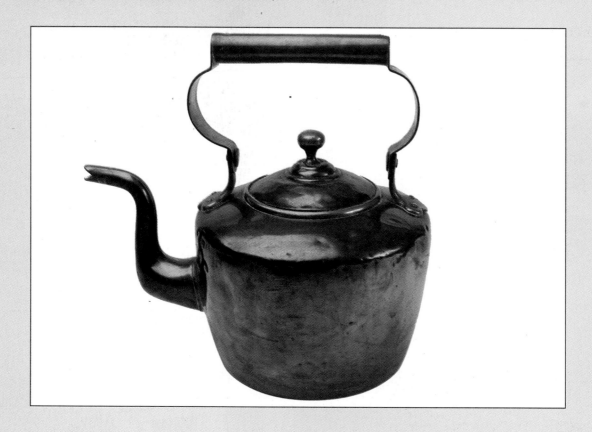

1890s
This kettle is made of copper. The kettle was put on top of the range. The heat from the range boiled the water.

18

1920s

A metal bar inside the kettle was heated by electricity. The hot metal bar heated the water. Someone had to watch the kettle and switch it off when the water had boiled.

Now

This is a cordless kettle. It can be lifted off its stand and carried around. When the kettle boils, a special switch turns the kettle off.

Milk bottles

People have used all sorts of things to carry milk from the dairy to the home.

1890s

This is a pottery milk pail.
It has a copper lid.

1930s
Dairies began delivering milk in bottles.
This bottle has a cardboard lid.

Now
We can buy milk from supermarkets
and shops too.
This milk is in a plastic container.

Pans

We cook food in pans on a cooker.

1890s

This pan is made from copper. It is lined
with tin because eating food that has
been cooked next to copper could make
you very ill.

1930s

This is an enamel pan.
Enamel is a special sort of paint which
doesn't crack when it is heated.

Now

This pan has a non-stick coating inside.
This makes the pan very easy to clean
because food does not stick to the sides.

Telephones

We use telephones to speak to other people over short and long distances.

1910s

This telephone does not have a dial or numbers to press. Instead you had to call the **operator** who would put you through to the person you wanted to speak to.

1920s

This is one of the first telephones with a dial.

1950s

Telephones were this shape for a long time. For many years, all telephones were black.

Now

The handpiece of this telephone does not even have to be connected to the rest of the phone! It means you can talk to your friends while walking around the house.

Radios

We use radios to listen to sounds sent out from radio stations.

1930s
The first radios people listened to were very large. This was because the parts inside the radios were big. The radio in the photograph is sometimes called a valve radio.

1970s

Scientists found a way of making the parts inside the radio smaller and so the radio itself got smaller. This type of radio was known as a transistor radio.

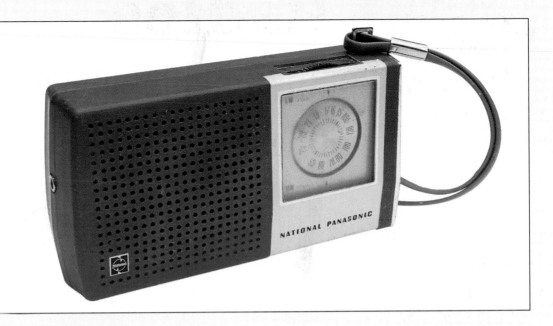

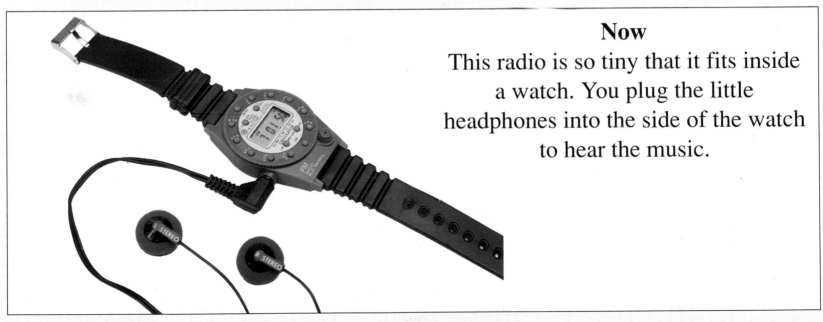

Now

This radio is so tiny that it fits inside a watch. You plug the little headphones into the side of the watch to hear the music.

Sewing machines

We use sewing machines to sew bits of material to make clothes or curtains.

1920s

This sewing machine was worked by hand. One hand had to turn the handle while the other hand moved the material. The machine could only sew straight stitches.

Now

Here is a modern sewing machine. It can sew zig-zag stitches as well as straight stitches. The sewing machine works by electricity. The machine goes when a pedal on the floor is pressed. This leaves both hands free to move the material.

Glossary

clamped fastened or fixed

frame the main shape of something

grate a small basket made of metal bars

hob the top part of a cooker

ingredients all the different foods used in cooking

magnet a special metal that other metals stick to

materials what objects are made of

operator someone who works for a telephone company

prongs the pointed parts of a fork

settings the controls that let you choose how hot or cold you want something to be, or how long you want something to work for

1860s	1870s	1880s	1890s	1900s	1910s	1920s

Books to read

History From Photographs series by Kath Cox and Pat Hughes (Wayland, 1995-6)
How We Used To Live, 1902-1926 by Freda Kelsall (A & C Black, 1985)
How We Used To Live, 1954-1970 by Freda Kelsall (A & C Black, 1987)
People Through History series by Karen Bryant-Mole (Wayland, 1996)
Starting History series by Stewart Ross (Wayland, 1991)

The illustration below is a timeline. The black and white drawings are of all the objects you have seen photographed in this book. Use the timeline to work out which objects came earlier or later than others, and which were around at the same time.

1930s	1940s	1950s	1960s	1970s	1980s	now

Index

Acknowledgements
The Publishers would like to thank the following Organizations, which supplied the objects used in this book: By courtesy of the Royal Pavilion, Art Gallery and Museums (Preston Manor), Brighton 4, 6, 8, 10 (left), 13, 14, 16, 17 (left), 18, 20, 25 (left), 22, 24 (both); Buckley's Yesterday's World, Battle, East Sussex 5 (left), 12, 26; Norfolk Museums Service 9 (top), 19 (left), 23 (top). All photographs are by Zul Mukhida except for those on pages 9 (top), 19 (left), 23 (top), which are by GGS Photographics.